In the Weedy Rock Pool

Helena Ramsay

Illustrated by
Lynda Stevens

Evans

We're at the seaside.

The tide has gone out.

4

Let's go and look in the rock pools.

5

Here's a big rock pool. What's that scuttling into the water?

That's a crab. It's running sideways.

A crab has eight legs and a pair of
pincers in front for catching and
holding its food.
Its shell is tough like a suit of armour.

7

Ouch, my feet hurt!

The rocks are very sharp.

These rocks are covered with barnacles. When the tide comes in barnacles open their shells and their long, feathery legs come out.

Barnacles use their legs for catching tiny bits of food in the water.

It's fun looking in rock pools, but it would be even better to shrink in size and swim under the water.

This is fantastic!

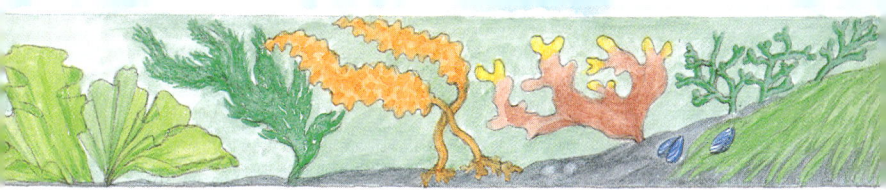

The seaweed has got bubbles in it.

I like to pop them.

It's called bladderwrack. The air bubbles help it to float in the water.

Look, there's a fish.

Where's it gone?

It's a little fish called a blenny. It has been hiding from us like all the other creatures.

12

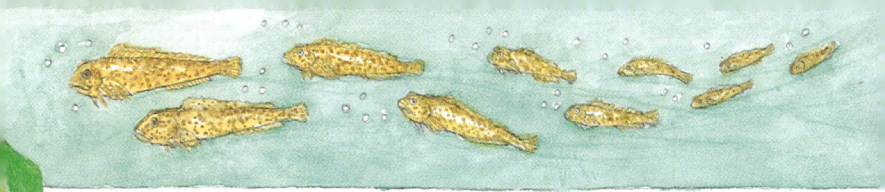

Its speckled markings made it look
like a stone or the sand on
the bottom of the pool.

13

Look at that starfish.

It's coming this way.
Help, will it eat us?

14

No, starfish eat shellfish. They wrap themselves around the shells and force them open. Then they eat the creature inside.

What's that?

It looks like a hedgehog.

That's a sea-urchin. It's covered in spines to protect it from seagulls or other hungry creatures.

It uses its strong jaws to scrape
food off the rocks.

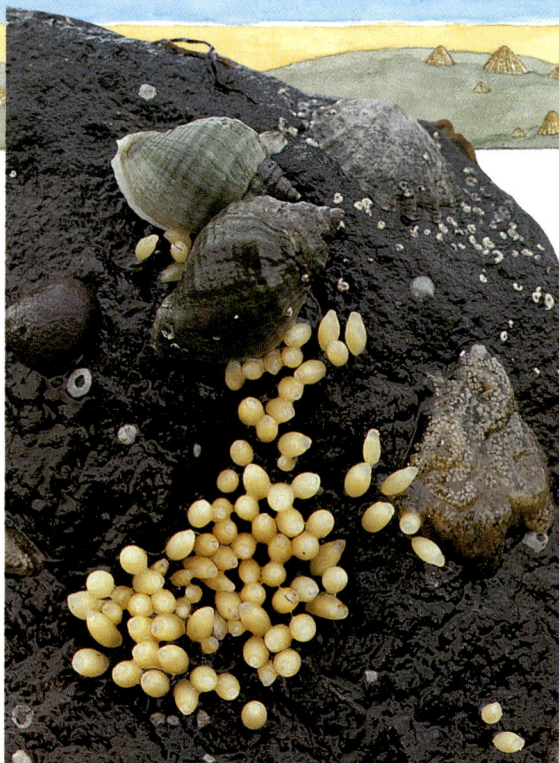

Who lives in these shells?

Those are dog whelks. Those little yellow pods on the rock are their eggs.

18

I can't get this one off the rock. What is it?

It's a limpet. It uses a sucker under its body to stick to the rock. It clings to the rock so that it can't be eaten by hungry seagulls or hurt by the waves.

19

There's another whelk.

No it isn't.
It's got long legs!

It's a hermit crab. It has no shell of
its own and so it has found an empty
whelk shell to live in.

As it grows it has to find larger and larger shells to move into.

Look at those flowers. Aren't they pretty.

They're not flowers, they are sea-anemones.
Those petals are really tentacles. Let's
not go too close, they have a nasty sting
that they use to poison their prey.

Look at that prawn.

Help, it's going much too close to the anemone!

Now it's been caught!

For many creatures in the rock pool life is very dangerous. They always have to be on their guard.

25

26

27

Look at this picture. How many of these things can you name? The answers are on the next page but don't peep until you have tried yourself.

7

3

5

1

29

The pictures in this book show many animals much bigger than they really are. This is their real size compared to you.

Blenny

Crab

Sea-anemone

30